FROM GENER
TO GENERA

The all-embracing
family of God

FROM GENERATION TO GENERATION

The all-embracing family of God

by

Robert and Janet Street

Salvation Books
The Salvation Army International Headquarters
London, United Kingdom

First published 2008

Copyright © 2008
The General of The Salvation Army

ISBN 978 0 85412 781 8

Cover design by Nathan Sigauke

Published by Salvation Books
The Salvation Army International Headquarters
101 Queen Victoria Street, London EC4V 4EH, United Kingdom

Printed by UK Territory Print & Design Unit

Contents

Preface

The Salvation Army family

The Salvation Army is part of the family of God. It is also a family in its own right – one that keeps growing, and stretches round the world. Its common goals and global unity speak of the creative and healing power of God in a hurting world. They show the love of Jesus Christ in action, making a difference, everywhere.

This family is for people of all ages, all nations and every social standing. Everyone may belong. Even those who haven't joined may feel part of it. In fact, the Army exists for them, because it exists for 'others'.

The Salvation Army family has its own God-given role to play in the world. To achieve this to the best effect, every generation has to play its part. Each has opportunities every day and everywhere to support, learn from and teach each other – and to love one another.

From Generation to Generation is produced to show that loving connectedness between the generations is rooted in Scripture and is God's will for his world. It is hoped the book will also ensure that no generation's needs or contributions are overlooked.

Robert and Janet Street
Commissioners
London, United Kingdom
May 2008

Generation Next

'Let this be written for a future generation, that a people not yet created may praise the Lord' (Psalm 102:18, *New International Version*).

A Prayer . . .

… that far-reaching and spiritually-enriching outcomes will be achieved from this study through the discussions and sharing that take place, with each generation contributing to the health, growth and witness of the family of God.

Introduction

'His mercy extends to those who fear him,
from generation to generation' (Luke 1:50)

When Mary was told the news that she was to become a mother – and not just any mother, but the mother of the Son of God – she set an example for every generation. With simple, uncomplicated acceptance, she replied: 'I am the Lord's servant. May it be to me as you have said' (Luke 1:38 – all quotations from *New International Version*). It was total surrender. Complete obedience to God's will.

Mary was to be entrusted with a young, precious life: Jesus. He would develop naturally like any other child and grow 'in wisdom and stature, and in favour with God and men' (Luke 2:51). He needed a good mother to care for and teach him.

At the end of his life Jesus was found in the Garden of Gethsemane displaying the same attitude as his mother and effectively with the same prayer on his lips. Battling against the temptation to back out of giving his life on the Cross, he prayed: 'Father, if you are willing, take this cup from me; yet not my will, but yours be done' (Luke 22:42). It was total surrender. Complete obedience to his Father's will.

During his ministry, when asked for teaching about prayer, Jesus placed God's will right at its centre for us too. 'Your will be done on earth as it is in Heaven' (Matthew 6:10), he taught.

As we look at Mary and Jesus we see that foundation principles for every family were being passed on 'from generation to generation' – a phrase which Mary used as she responded with joy to the honour of being God's servant (Luke 1:50).

Scores of generations later, each of us has opportunity to do God's will, to embrace and cherish it, and pass it on to the next generation.

From generation to generation!

Chapter 1

From generation to generation

'These commandments that I give you today are to be upon your hearts. Impress them on your children. Talk about them when you sit at home and when you walk along the road, when you lie down and when you get up' (Deuteronomy 6:6,7).

IN many developed countries, life expectancy has increased to such an extent that there are now more generations living together than at any other time in history. It is becoming normal for people to live to an age that brings them great-grandchildren and, for an increasing number, great-great-grandchildren.

The preferences, customs and lifestyles of the generations can vary enormously, and when those same generations are living in an age of unprecedented change, the tensions and challenges of living in harmony are magnified. The pace of change is now so swift that one generation doesn't have time to identify itself before more rapid change has overtaken it.

In his award-winning book, *The Dignity of Difference*, Dr Jonathan Sacks looks at this issue: 'Something happens when change is so rapid that nothing confers meaning – when lives become lifestyles, commitments become experiments, relationships become provisional, careers turn into contracts, and life itself ceases to have the character of a narrative and becomes instead a series of episodes with no connecting thread.'

Countries still struggling to develop also face changes, though at times their situations are often dramatically and radically different. Life expectancy is sometimes less than half that found in the Western world, with millions of children orphaned through HIV/Aids or because of other modern social phenomena. In such places the part played by extended family through the generations is deeply significant.

In the Western world, prolific Australian author and social researcher, Dr Hugh McKay, points to four major dimensions of life which have undergone dramatic upheaval, bringing about cultural revolution and permeating all levels of society. He identifies the dimensions as gender, economy, technology and identity.

The cultural revolution has brought with it widespread decline in commitment – to marriage, society in general, work, institutions, long-term relationships, the Church, and to God. This less than dutiful approach to life leaves people of all ages scrambling to find their place or 'home' in the world, and searching for a sense of self-worth or personal well-being. With no real sense of where change is taking us, the effects are seen in a variety of guises. In Australia, for instance, consumption of anti-depressants has tripled in the past 10 years. In Ireland, Japan and New Zealand suicide rates among the young have soared.

There is a growing disconnectedness between generations. Because of the number of breakdowns in relationships, generational interaction becomes a casualty. The youth section of society tends to retreat from relating to older generations, and peer pressure, or peer culture, takes over – at times with disastrous results.

The elderly are belittled, humoured or marginalised. Their potential contribution to other generations – wisdom, experience, support and friendship – is all too often overlooked or not recognised.

While all this is going on, the middle-aged are pressurised from all sides – work demands, children, elderly parents, finance – and young adults seem reluctant to venture outside their immediate circle of friends and responsibilities. Many spend or borrow beyond their means, unsure that there will be a tomorrow.

In some places churches have fallen into the trap of thinking that generations can only be managed separately. They have arranged activities and worship which encourage polarisation rather than interaction. Supposing that the gaps between generations are too wide to fill, they have neglected the building of true family worship and understanding, with all their mutual benefits. They have followed 'the trend', not daring to believe the trend can be changed.

But it is our differences that give us identity and worth. It is our differences which are our gift to others. We shouldn't run away from them, or write them off as being unwelcome, unwanted or unhelpful. Different generations can enrich each other immeasurably. The less frantic countries of the world seem to understand this so much better.

Jesus spoke in family terms. He spoke of love from a Heavenly Father. He talked of acceptance, forgiveness and welcome. As Son of God, he chose to become our brother and live among us. His life and teaching touched all generations when he was on earth. They still touch them.

The genealogies at the beginning of the Gospels of Matthew and Luke show that the family and nation into which Jesus was born had succeeded in passing on the faith through the generations. They had seen it as a sacred trust and command (Deuteronomy 6:4–9). Since the time of Jesus, Christian faith has been communicated through the generations.

It isn't unusual for a Jew to speak in favour of faith being passed on through generations, but speaking on the BBC in London, Dr Jonathan Sacks, as Chief Rabbi, spoke strongly of the need for Britain to retain its Christian faith. Emphasising that the 'real victories' in any nation's life are spiritual, he said: 'What sustains a nation is its culture and its faith, and the way it hands them on across the generations.' He continued: 'Empires have come and gone . . . faith survives: and the only societies that have endured for long have been held together by a sense of the sacred.' If this is true for nations and societies, it is also true for The Salvation Army.

Commissioner Helen Clifton, as World President of Women's Ministries, recently called Salvationists to consider their responsibilities to the next generation – 'how to be godly role models, teachers and protectors of young people'. Example is significant and effective.

The Salvation Army dates back only to 1865 when William Booth began his mission on Mile End Waste. In comparison with the total history of the Church it isn't very long – just a few generations. Perhaps this is why Salvationists sometimes mention that they are third, fourth or fifth-generation Salvationists. Maybe, without realising it, they want to emphasise the continuing nature of the Movement, its stability and ongoing effectiveness.

It isn't unusual to hear people warn of the dangers of merely 'depending on your parents' experience of God' rather than being sure of your own personal relationship with Jesus Christ. The warning has its value. However well anyone has been taught the gospel, ultimately we are each responsible for inviting Christ into our lives and making our own commitment to him.

But shouldn't there also be a strong note of thanksgiving every time we hear young Salvationists – especially new soldiers – speaking of their heritage with holy pride? We are witnessing the praiseworthy evidence that passing on the faith 'from generation to generation' is working.

When children 'brought up' in the Army turn their back on their parents' faith we may justifiably feel a sense of loss and sorrow. We feel for the parents who had hoped and prayed their children would find the same joy as they do in serving Jesus. We instinctively want to support them in their hopes that the seeds of faith sown in childhood will eventually flower.

It is time to strengthen our intention to guide and encourage each generation into faith – and soldiership. It is a worthy ambition. It is a holy one too. When the faith of the Church is embraced we praise God. It is evidence of the teaching of the years being shared, understood and received.

The postmodern world has brought new opportunities for connecting with people outside the Church, but it has also discouraged many in the Church from believing that commitment to God is still likely or even possible. Some have allowed themselves to lose confidence in the promise stated by Jesus – that if we lose our life for his sake we will find it (Mark 8:35). But the truth of these words has been proved time and time again, century after century. Those who throw in their lot with Jesus Christ, embracing his radical self-giving example, receive more from him than they either deserve or could imagine.

This age requires boldness. It is an age for recovering confidence – for the family of The Salvation Army to play its divinely-commissioned part in passing on the faith.

From generation to generation!

For discussion

▲ Read Deuteronomy 6:4-9 and note the commands given by God to his people for passing on the faith through the generations. What instructions were given to the people in order to do this? What do the verses tell us about the importance of passing on the faith?

▲ Read again verse 6. What does it tell you specifically?

▲ How different is our world from that of previous generations?

▲ What are the 21st century challenges in general and for the Army in particular? How can they be met?

Chapter 2

Family identity

'Yet to all who received him, to those who believed in his name, he gave the right to become children of God' (John 1:12).

WHEN Jesus asked his disciples, 'Who do people say that I am?' (Mark 8:27) the answers varied. Before leaving the remote region of Caesarea Philippi to take the long road to Jerusalem and the Cross, Jesus wanted an update on how he had been identified.

The response of the disciples showed that people's perceptions were on the right track: 'Some say John the Baptist; others say Elijah; and still others, one of the prophets' (v 28). He had been identified as a man of God. But something was still lacking. People hadn't quite got it right.

Twenty-first century research across a variety of cultures, asking the public 'What is The Salvation Army?' brings a similar result. Some identify the Army as a Christian social movement, some just as a social organisation (though perhaps with a religious conviction), some as a church with a social conscience, some have no idea, while others see it primarily as an evangelical movement. There are other perceptions, of course, and they vary from culture to culture.

These findings are to be expected. In the same way that people had an idea who Jesus was, so they have their opinions about the Army. It's simply a fact of life that people have their own inbuilt bias, their personal interests, and areas of their mind which are closed to anything that doesn't interest them.

Any random group listening to the same news bulletin will hear and register some items – and ignore others. Our individual perception of each item will also vary according to our prior knowledge and understanding of the subject in question – not to mention our temperament, optimism (or lack of it) and convictions. The Salvation Army is assessed on the same basis.

It's unlikely that Jesus was alarmed or surprised by the answers he received. He was probably more interested in the answers to his next question. It was directed at his closest followers, his disciples: 'But what about you?' he asked. 'Who do you say I am?' (v 29). The answer came immediately from the lips of Peter: 'You are the Christ.'

Someone had got it right! Having established that – with his closest followers now knowing who he was – Jesus was ready to reveal himself more fully to others.

The Salvation Army's most important question may not be 'Who do people think we are?' (though we want them to get it right). Far more crucial is: 'What do *we* who bear the name Salvationist think the Army is? If *we* don't know, how can we expect others to know – and what kind of family would we imagine we were inviting others to join? We need to know – and to know that we know.

A few years ago, a cadet couple were being interviewed by the Principal in his office at William Booth College, London, when the husband was asked why he had left another denomination to become a Salvationist. He thought for a few moments and then replied with a smile on his face: 'I like the Army because, even when we aren't doing what we should be doing, we still know what we should be doing.' What did he mean?

He was intimating that Salvationists instinctively know what being a Salvationist means – even if sometimes they fail to live out its ideals and disciplines as well as they might hope. Although actions may not always match promises, the family identity – its message and mission – is not in doubt.

In recent years, General John Gowans helped us express ourselves in clear, concise words. 'We exist,' he said, 'to save souls, grow saints and serve suffering humanity.'

He made it sound simple. And so it is. We *instinctively know* these words take us right to the heart of the Army – to who we are – to our identity. The Salvation Army family exists to bring others to know God as their Father and Jesus as their Saviour. It exists to help all who belong to grow in their relationship with God, to know him as their guiding companion and strength-giver. And it is also fundamental to the family that its caring arms reach out to everyone, whatever their race, religion, reputation or relationships.

The ways in which we undertake these three expressions of our one identity will vary, but let's not suppose that because we give expression to our faith in numerous ways we have an identity crisis. It's just not so – or needn't be. How we express who we are should regularly be adapted to suit times and situations – but always with the firm understanding of our unalterable underlying three-fold God-given mission.

Jesus knew that he had (and was) what the world needed. It mattered to him that his followers knew it and believed it too. Surrounded by people – good and bad – who wanted to change his mind and mission, he refused to be swayed or sidetracked. It is the same for the Army. From time to time, and in differing locations, some Salvationists seem unsure of what the Army should be, and then, through their own lack of confidence, cause confusion in others. It is then we must have the same underlying resolve and confidence as Jesus – confidence in the identity he gives us – because the surest way to an identity crisis is to let yourself be talked into one.

Essentially, The Salvation Army's identity comes from the same source as other Christian expressions of the faith. The Army is part of the Body of Christ (1 Corinthians 12:12). It belongs to and with other Christians. It traces its beginnings back through history to a stable in Bethlehem, a cross on Calvary and an empty Jerusalem tomb. Its identity comes from Jesus and in being united with all Christians by his Holy Spirit (v 13).

Not surprisingly, the family of God has identifiable family characteristics. As children may look or act like their parents or siblings, so children of God find there are characteristics that not only identify them, but unite them too.

There were occasions when Jesus gave specific examples of how he expected God's children to act or react. In the Sermon on the Mount he taught his disciples to 'Love your enemies, bless those who curse you, do good to those who hate you and pray for those who persecute you' (Matthew 5:44). This, he said, would make them sons (or children) of their Father in Heaven (v 45).

Because Christians see Jesus as their supreme example, they try to be like him. They see in his life qualities to be emulated. He promised his Spirit to help us in this, so we can use the 'fruit' of that Spirit – recorded by the Apostle Paul in Galatians 5:22 – as a good reference point for how we should be developing spiritually. The fruit of the Spirit is listed as love, joy, peace, patience, kindness, goodness, faithfulness, gentleness and self-control. These characteristics should be increasingly evident in all Christians. They identify God's family – the people who are linked with him by the Holy Spirit's presence in their lives.

Salvationists share other family characteristics. The structure of the Army, songs written by its poets, doctrines which all soldiers embrace, sacred music gifted to the movement by its composers, the readiness to be identified with one another by wearing uniform, public testimony in meetings, prayerful use of the mercy seat and the belief that the whole of life should be lived as a sacrament to God – these are some of the things that bind Salvationists together and give them their shared identity.

It is a family within the family of God. It is not made up of perfect people – but that's the reason why we can all belong.

For discussion

▲ Discuss what identifies us as children of God.

▲ Share your personal perceptions of the Army as a family of God.

▲ What can be done to improve general perceptions about the Army and why it exists?

▲ What are the unifying factors in your corps? How well are the three aims of the Army – to save souls, grow saints and serve suffering humanity – balanced locally?

Chapter 3

'Fearfully and wonderfully made'

'For you created my inmost being; you knit me together in my mother's womb. I praise you because I am fearfully and wonderfully made; your works are wonderful' (Psalm 139:13, 14).

WE are intricate creatures. Scientists have unravelled an incredible amount of information about our bodies, but there is always more to discover.

We're told that 50,000 cells in our body will die and be replaced with new cells in the time it takes to read this sentence. Every individual of the more than six billion world population not only has a unique DNA, but also unique tongue prints and finger prints. The way in which each intricate part of our body works in harmony with countless other parts suggests something more than an accident of nature. It was beyond the psalmist's understanding (Psalm 139:6). Even with all our increasing knowledge, it is beyond ours too.

When we recognise the complexity of the brain, the range of possible emotions, each unique personality and our capacity for making rational decisions based on logic, feelings and circumstances, it isn't difficult to agree with the psalmist's shout of praise – 'I am fearfully and wonderfully made' (Psalm 139:14).

Such intricate detail means we are also sensitive, vulnerable, unpredictable, ever learning and developing. We need handling with care. We seek acceptance and a sense of worth – because they are essential to our well-being. We can't isolate ourselves from

13

others and still retain any true sense of being or belonging. We need each other for interaction. We need love.

We also have the capacity for greatness and notoriety, for goodness and evil, for success and failure. We are capable of achieving much that is either worthy and enriching, or unworthy and destructive. When we touch each other's lives our actions affect not only our own spirit and circumstances but also those of others. Sometimes this works well, at other times it does lasting damage. None of us is exempt from the effects of mutual contact.

Also, none of us is perfect. Not one of us is complete, or without weakness or fault of some kind. Some of us are born with disease or deformity that can be readily identified. Others encounter challenges through the years or become aware of our shortcomings as we meet specific circumstances. Sometimes we don't feel as 'wonderful' as the psalmist suggests. Our imperfections bring questions with them. We may resent them, but none of us is without imperfection of some kind and all of us have the challenge as to how we live with them – both ours and those of others.

Significantly, the hardships, difficulties and challenges of life are the means by which we develop as people. We learn more about ourselves as we face unwelcome realities. Body, mind and spirit frequently combine to achieve the unachievable – and we discover something more of why we were made and who we are.

As individuals we are defined by our differences. Our uniqueness gives us our identity. The ever-changing face of society – in gender roles, economic climate, technological progress, lifestyle, relationships – has made underlying permanent identity less easy to define. In consequence, we are told, we look for aspects of our lives that we can control, disengaging from areas of life that might threaten or belittle us. There is a tendency to turn inward only to find that we become obsessed with do-it-yourself projects, personal possessions and financial securities, with less interaction in community – but without interaction our identity means very little.

Integral to all this is the Christian belief that we are each made in the image of God. The Bible uses the word 'made', as in Psalm 139, without a second thought. In the first chapter of the first book, God is recorded as saying: 'Let us *make* man in our image' (Genesis 1:26). They are the words of a creator, our Creator. They speak of intention, of design, of purpose. The activity of God is taken for granted. Any suggestion that there is not a designing, creating God is seen as foolish (Psalm 14:1).

Scripture consistently shows that we belong in relationship with God and, because we are his creatures, in relationship with each other (Psalm 42). For life to have personal meaning we need to have people who matter to us and the knowledge that we matter to others.

On one famous occasion (recorded in Matthew 18), Jesus suggested that when we look into the face of a child we should actually be able to see him (v 5). He said that when we welcome anyone we are receiving him. We are to look for and respect the image of God in each other. It is beyond our capacity to look directly into the face of God (Exodus 33:20), but he has made it possible for us to recognise him in each other. We don't always manage this very well.

Augustine put our existence into its essential context. 'Thou hast made us for thyself; O Lord,' he wrote, 'and our hearts are restless until they find their rest in thee.' Each tiny life that arrives in our world is born to know God, to have relationship with him – to discover that we are his children and that we are dearly loved.

God's framework for relationship was there when the first commandments were given through Moses to the Israelite nation. As we have already noted, the people were told to love God with all their 'heart, soul and strength' (Deuteronomy 6:5) and their neighbour as themselves (Leviticus 18:19).

God's framework of love is the framework for life, so it is to be passed on from generation to generation with passion and purpose (Deuteronomy 6:7-9).

The deliberate passing on of truth, tradition and moral guidance is viewed more importantly by some families than others. Some parents find it difficult to be intimate about sacred things, while others have such a disrupted timetable in their home – with family members coming, going and eating at different times – that a structured approach to teaching or even sharing one another's company is non-existent, or rarely achieved. Salvation Army families (in the home or at the corps), by their very nature, are usually busy. There is a danger that in the 'doing', the reason for 'being' a family is overlooked. Sometimes it is taken for granted in a secure, loving way. At other times it leads to dysfunctional behaviour and lack of real motivation.

Whoever we are, time to reflect on the fact that we are 'fearfully and wonderfully made' will help us get our own lives in perspective. We are precious to God – each one of us. By making us in his image, capable of having relationship with him, he is letting us know that we are capable of more than mere existence or passing importance.

Galileo is reported to have said that the sun, with all the planets revolving around it and dependent on it, is able to ripen one bunch of grapes as if it was the only thing in the world it had to do. The same can be said of God's love for each individual in his creation.

We are fearfully and wonderfully made with eternity in mind. The Psalm which reminds us of this concludes with the prayer: 'Search me, O God, and know my heart; test me and know my anxious thoughts. See if there is any offensive way in me, and lead me in the way everlasting' (Psalm 139:23, 24).

Albert Frederick Bayly puts our humanity into divine perspective:

You, Lord, have stamped your image on your creatures,
And, though they mar that image, love them still;
Lift up our eyes to Christ, that in his features
We may discern the beauty of your will.
            (*The Song Book of The Salvation Army,* Number 38)

God has made us for relationship – with himself, and forever.
All our relationships should bear this in mind and find us working
for each other's good – from generation to generation.

For discussion

▲ In addition to being 'fearfully and wonderfully made', the psalmist acknowledges that God made 'our inmost being' (Psalm 139:13, 14). What does this say about:
  the kind of creatures we are;
  our capacity for relationship with God?

▲ How well does the way we relate to others reflect our relationship with God?

▲ 'God's framework of love is the framework for life.' Discuss what this means.

▲ How can we achieve a good balance between 'being' and 'doing' as Salvationists?

Chapter 4

Welcome to our world

'And whoever welcomes a little child like this in my name
welcomes me' (Matthew 18:5).

THE welcome awaiting any newborn baby is unique. The people who will care for the child and the circumstances into which it is born always vary. No two parents are the same. No two homes are alike in every way. Families come in all shapes and sizes. Some have two parents, others have one. Some babies are born into step or 'blended' families, or perhaps extended families. In a growing number of countries gay and lesbian families have become increasingly accepted. Some families trying to adjust to the arrival of a 'new mouth to feed' are homeless or destitute.

The world outside the front door – if there is a front door – is constantly changing. It would be near impossible to find any city or town in the world where the landscape isn't being rearranged – either with skyscrapers, shopping malls, roads and highways, or some other new facility.

Sometimes the landscape changes because of disaster or deprivation. The possibility of global catastrophe seems to loom larger than at any previous time in history. Fears of nuclear warfare, health scares and global epidemics compete for news headlines with terrorist activity and the unpredictability of climate change. What the future holds, nobody knows for certain. Even the most informed predictions – on whatever subject – seem to be flawed, and science itself is constantly found changing its mind on 'established facts'.

It had been anticipated by some that religion would lose its attraction or power, but it hasn't. It is at the heart of all that is best and sometimes all that is worst in human nature. Reactions to religion and the embracing of faith take many forms. Christians, Muslims, Hindus and Buddhists make up the world's four most prolific religions (in that order), but a newborn child is likely to find many more expressions of faith to choose from. Some estimates suggest there are at least 500 million non-believers in the world – which would, in fact, make atheism the fourth biggest 'religion'.

A major issue for churches in developing countries is the strength of generational influences within culture and religions that are not compatible with Christianity. Deciding and then teaching what is and isn't appropriate to retain in culture must be achieved with clarity and care. Rejecting customs which have been part of a nation's infrastructure presents particular challenges.

Among the most significant changes affecting modern homes is lifestyle. With women now having a radically different view of their status and role, the institution of marriage has been transformed. Spouses have struggled with the challenge of making adjustments and their confusion has had far-reaching consequences. The divorce rate has soared and the birth rate has plummeted. There is less stability.

With abortion having become so readily available throughout the world, some newborn babies don't know how close they came to not arriving at all. The sanctity of human life can't be taken for granted. Even the most 'civilised' societies seem oblivious at times to the obligation to protect the vulnerable.

On the other hand, health services and the possibility of cures for 'incurable' illnesses have increased dramatically. The harnessing of different energies and technological progress has brought comfort, security and a quality and standard of living previously unknown. Opportunities for progress in education, health and self-fulfilment seem endless. Transport and global communication have never been better. New opportunities for leisure and pleasure are waiting to be explored.

If you are born in the right place at the right time, life will look promising. But with a small privileged percentage of the world owning the larger percentage of the world's riches there are more babies seemingly born in the wrong place, at the wrong time and in the wrong circumstances. Health services, education, safety from abuse and harm, and provision of clean water are unavailable to hundreds of millions. The universal culture change required to see the human family working for each other's united good seems overwhelming.

What is The Salvation Army's response to this? What does it offer a new-born baby that will help the child not only adjust to its environment and circumstances, but also make its own contribution?

On a practical level it offers education to almost 500,000 children daily. Its wide-ranging health services, rescue homes for abandoned children, protection policies and parenting programmes make their impact on all continents, but the needs are always greater than available resources.

What The Salvation Army offers above all is a family – not a perfect family, but a family into which a new life may be welcomed. Whether orphaned, abandoned, born into a divided or loving home, every child deserves to be welcomed into a family made up of people who know they are equally loved by God, and that he has no favourites. The Salvation Army family is a family that has its foundation in the belief that everyone is made in the image of God and as such deserves respect, acceptance and genuine care.

Putting these ideals into practice requires commitment and sensitivity. The variety of needs presented by the complexity of differing family circumstances is hugely challenging. If The Salvation Army is to make any impact at all, it has to be flexible, non-judgmental and welcoming; prepared to engage with people at their point of need.

The 'official' welcome to a child is most clearly seen in the provision of a dedication ceremony. The ceremony is faith based and rooted in life values. It is a ceremony in which the baby is publicly introduced to the congregation – the family of God's people who belong to the local Salvation Army corps.

As any baby is too young to make promises of its own, the parents take the initiative. After thanking God for the gift of 'this precious life', the parents promise – as far as they are able – to protect the child from everything that is likely to cause harm. They also promise to be good examples and to help their child grow in Christian faith and commitment. In short, the dedication ceremony provides a healthy, wholesome framework for life.

The people present at the ceremony are also invited to promise to pray for the child, and to offer support as the years go by. Everything that takes place points to shared commitment on behalf of the child, who will increasingly have opportunity to develop a sense of commitment too.

This is the beginning. The acceptance, support and nurture given by the Army family will (hopefully) be rewarded by seeing the child's character develop positively. Later it will be complemented by its growing contribution as year succeeds year.

Significantly, The Salvation Army also offers a thanksgiving ceremony as an alternative for parents who may not feel able to make the promises required in a dedication ceremony. Again, the important feature is that the child is welcomed into the life of the corps. This family is for everyone.

Whatever the circumstances into which the child is born, regardless of the qualities of the parent or parents, in spite of social challenges, the acceptance of the child publicly highlights its arrival and welcome into the world. To further acknowledge this, the child's name may be added to the cradle roll. It may be the first social group to which the child belongs, but it is a good one. It is wholesome. It is an early, active experience of the love of God.

After the dedication ceremony is over, and once the congregation has gone home, the task of keeping promises begins. No parent, however determined, will manage always to be the example he or she wishes to be. There will be moments of failure and disappointment. Members of the congregation, in spite of their hopes for the child, need to accept the fact that the environment which they create in the Salvation Army corps will have a profound effect on the child. The child may learn either love and acceptance or hypocrisy and self-interest. First impressions are profound.

No Salvation Army corps family will ever be perfect. How can it be if it is open to us all? But we can each do our part to help it be as representative as possible of the family of God – and to be as welcoming of any new child as Mary was of the Son of God.

For discussion

▲ What are the implications of Jesus' statement that 'whoever welcomes a little child . . . in my name welcomes me' (Matthew 18:5)?

▲ Discuss how welcome you feel in your own world.

▲ In a world that has unwelcoming aspects, how do you see the Army family playing a significant role in your area?

▲ How would you describe the environment that has been created in your corps family? What could be done to make it more welcoming?

Chapter 5

First steps

'And Jesus grew in wisdom and stature, and in favour with God and men' (Luke 2:52).

IT isn't only the new arrival into the family who has to learn to take first steps. Parents welcoming their first child have to take their first steps too – in parenting. However keenly the baby's birth was anticipated, and however thorough preparations may have been, the new parents' life has changed. They are responsible for a life, somebody else's life – a dependent, vulnerable life – their child's life.

They must ensure this young life is fed, kept warm, clothed and sheltered. They must 'handle with care' in every way. Keeping the baby safe from physical harm, watching over it and responding to its needs, are all aspects of a new and more demanding lifestyle. Some new parents are more able to adjust than others. Some seem completely taken by surprise, and flounder.

The help available varies from family to family, country to country, culture to culture. Some cultures seem better equipped to embrace the new-born child into the security of the extended family, while new parents in other cultures can find themselves alone, and in need of moral and physical support. If a new mother is alone, pressures can be overwhelming.

We can only try to imagine how Mary and Joseph felt about being given responsibility to care for Jesus, whom, they were told, would be the Saviour of the world. Having never been a mother before, the young Mary would have been glad of the support of the

25

older Joseph, but even he was taking on a kind of responsibility he could never have envisaged.

Luke's Gospel tells us that during her pregnancy Mary kept in contact with her older cousin Elizabeth (1:39), who was also expecting her first child – later to become known as John the Baptist. The family network was proving supportive, with each ensuring they sought the blessing and help of God in the raising of their child (1:66 and 2:28). From their earliest days, John and Jesus were introduced to the ways and laws of God. They were to grow up with them as naturally as they would grow up with dates and palm trees. Luke 2:41-52 shows us how Jesus was immersed in God's will and ways as a boy.

Those biblical 'first steps' for parents and children, may seem a million miles away from many modern situations – but they are still a good guide for bringing security, direction and order to the early days of a new family.

We're told that the kind of emotional and moral development that takes place during the first three or four years of a child's life will have a lasting effect on how the child interacts with people in the future. Behaviour is learned, responses are formed and a sense of well-being is either lovingly experienced or sadly denied. The importance of parents caring for their children in ways which provide a strong and healthy foundation for the years ahead is often not readily appreciated. It is vital, otherwise damaging habits and values will be embraced which will prove difficult (though not impossible) to lose in later life.

The following words from 'Children learn what they live' by Dorothy Law Nolte, are both a warning and an encouragement. Negative outcomes are noted as the poem begins:

> *If a child lives with criticism, he learns to condemn.*
> *If a child lives with hostility, he learns to fight.*
> *If a child lives with fear, he learns to be apprehensive.*
> *If a child lives with pity, he learns to feel sorry for himself.*
> *If a child lives with ridicule, he learns to be shy.*

If a child lives with jealousy, he learns what envy is.
If a child lives with shame, he learns to feel guilty.

But good nurturing brings positive results.

If a child lives with encouragement, he learns to be confident.
If a child lives with tolerance, he learns to be patient.
If a child lives with praise, he learns to appreciate.
If a child lives with acceptance, he learns to love.
If a child lives with approval, he learns to like himself.

The message is clear. Those who lived with criticism as a child, or who never managed to achieve what their parents thought they should achieve, demand too much of themselves. They are never satisfied with their achievements, and in addition are likely to carry that demanding (and often harsh) nature into other relationships. They cause hurt by seldom giving affirmation or praise to those around them.

Children who live with fear or hostility bring a suspicious nature into adulthood. Unable to relax, they are prone to be on the attack before anyone else attacks them. People unable to 'take a joke' may well have been ridiculed by those closest to them, causing them to overreact to harmless fun. Cynical attitudes to life are learned from one generation to another, as is a sense of helplessness, or readiness to blame others when things go wrong.

Conversely, positive nurturing in a strong and caring environment has positive effects. It gives children a sense of self worth and of being valued. Although all the evidence points to the advantages of positive nurturing, many still seem reluctant to show warmth and affirmation, somehow managing to be unaware of their far-reaching value.

Because human nature is so complex, it is not always easy to distinguish between 'deliberate' bad parenting and a genuine sense of inadequacy. Nevertheless, all parents need help to some extent and in some form or another. Of all places, it should be available in a caring Christian fellowship.

In recent years there has been a surge in Salvation Army parent and toddler clubs, birthday clubs for toddlers, Baby Song groups, and the introduction of other programmes or events designed to bring parents together with their children. Baby Song has developed from being a popular Scandinavian initiative into an outreach programme now being embraced by an increasing number of Salvation Army territories.

Captain Anne Westmoreland, of the USA Southern Territory Women's Ministries team, explains something of the Baby Song's bonding opportunities for parent and child, as well as the benefits of meeting other new parents socially:

'The need for fellowship is a reality for many mothers (and fathers) of babies/toddlers, and it may not be easy to find a suitable environment to have that need met. Baby Song offers just that environment. It is a place where there is room for the baby/toddler, as well as for the parent to have interaction, parent-to-child, child-to-child and parent-to-parent. In addition to meeting social needs, Baby Song meets physical needs by offering activities that stimulate and develop the child physically. Spiritual needs are met through the chosen songs, as well as the interaction and openness for questions.'

A variety of toddler programmes – Baby Song included – can be particularly supportive to single parents, and their rapid growth is evidence of the relevance and usefulness of these initiatives. Groups such as these also help prepare children for full-time schooling. In countries where a place at school is not guaranteed, this kind of activity can have added significance because of the lack of educational or social opportunities.

Different ways of using the cradle roll (see chapter 4) to reach out into the community have been developed in many corps. The simple link of sending a birthday card during the first four years of a child's life has been used as a means of promoting more regular and supportive contact. Enterprising, creative social contact has been developed in many places. The huge responsibility of being a parent means there are always those who are only too glad to be part of wider social fellowship in which mutual support is naturally given. Any corps providing parenting classes needs to ensure that these are conducted appropriately and with expertise, but wherever they are held they play another vital part in helping new parents adjust to their roles.

The long-lasting benefit of activities for parents and toddlers may initially be appreciated only superficially, but the sense of well-being and development experienced within a secure and caring environment will reap rewards for life. Its effectiveness should never be underestimated. There are opportunities waiting to be taken.

For discussion

▲ Imagine and discuss how Mary and Joseph must have felt about the unique responsibility of helping Jesus grow 'in wisdom and stature, and in favour with God and men' (Luke 2:52). You may find it helpful to read the Introduction again in connection with this exercise.

▲ How aware are you of the early influences on your life and how they have influenced you?

▲ Negative and destructive attitudes are frequently passed from generation to generation. How can the cycle be broken or changed?

▲ Discuss and identify ways of reaching out to new parents in the culture of your community.

Chapter 6

'Mould me'

*'But if anyone causes one of these little ones who believe in me
to sin, it would be better for him to have a large millstone hung
around his neck and to be drowned in the depths of the sea'*
(Matthew 18:6).

THERE is no such thing as a self-made man or woman. Whatever
our achievements, and however much progress we have made,
none of us has accomplished anything entirely on our own. We
have all needed the help of other people at every stage in life.

In our early years, the influence of those who fed and clothed
us, and kept us safe, has to be acknowledged. Those who taught
us how to read, write and count have played their part in our life.
Others will have inspired us or given us self-belief. Some will have
taught us how to face crises or difficulties. We may even have
received money for our education from people who wanted us to
have the chance to 'do well'.

The support of governments and their programmes, the
community in which we live and the encouragement of friends all
add to our progress. Every moment of every day we are dependent
on the contribution of others, whether it is people whose books we
read, or whose technological equipment and systems we use, or
those who grow our food or help it arrive on our plate.

It's true there are negative sides to the influences on our lives
(as we have noted earlier), and these too have their way of shaping
the person we become. There may be people who we want
(justifiably) to blame for our lack of success, but this too merely

serves to emphasise that none of us is self-made. Influences upon our lives are always there – even when we aren't aware of them. We all owe a debt of gratitude to someone – to many people – for the support we have been given through life. On the other hand, there may be others we feel have hindered us.

Bearing this in mind, it makes sense to be careful as to how children are influenced. Early lessons and examples leave lasting impressions. Some communities understand this better than others. Parenting within the family is still strong in developing countries, but in Western society, with parents leading busy lives outside the home, much teaching that is foundational to life is either left to other people or overlooked.

Yet it would be misleading to suggest that influences outside the home are now more significant in the moulding of children's characters than those within the home. The music world, media, films, celebrity cult, reality TV shows, magazines and a multiplicity of internet connections profoundly affect children's thought patterns, values and priorities. These influences are invariably *inside* the home. They have found their way, courtesy of the technological revolution, into the heart of family life. The revolution is still taking place and is spreading to all cultures.

All this brings unprecedented challenges for parents. How can children be protected from dangerous influences when those same influences are an integral part of modern life? In addition to being accused of being too busy, parents may be either too harassed or careless to monitor what their children are doing or becoming involved in – especially in relation to communications through the internet.

Arguments over whether the media merely reflects today's morals – and responds to demand – or, because of its increasingly liberal output, is a major factor in promoting immoral practices, have been debated for the past few decades.

Another major issue is that parents also have been influenced. They are the product of their generation too, in which authority has been weakened and individuals invited to make up their own mind about morality and truth. A depressingly large percentage of some adult populations have little understanding of Christian faith, its values or the foundation it has given to society. Many are oblivious to its strengths and have a superficial concept of the place of religion in the world. There is much to be done if both children and adults are to overcome unthinking dismissive attitudes which hinder the embracing of values of the faith that have stood previous generations in good stead.

Overlooking foundational teaching means many children gain distorted concepts of some of life's aspects – sexuality, relationships and violence, for instance – before they have learned underlying values. In some cases the addiction of parents to drugs, gambling or alcohol means that children barely have a chance to avoid these pitfalls, setting a tragically negative pattern from which many never escape.

Computer games provide imaginative trips into 'virtual reality', but there is so much 'virtual' reality available that it isn't surprising that children don't always distinguish between what is real and what is not. Many prefer the virtual world as a distraction from the harsh reality in which they live.

The Salvation Army has a proven history of finding ways to prepare children for adulthood. It has been working in contrasting cultures for more than 100 years, adapting teaching and activities to age and circumstances, but always rooted in Scripture and the values taught by Jesus. At the heart of it all has been the combining of its influence on young lives with its responsibility to help them develop their own experience of God.

Perhaps the Army's most significant contribution for children has been (and still is) junior soldiership. From the age of seven, children are invited to become junior soldiers. It is a means by which they can make a simple commitment to Jesus Christ and promise (publicly) to follow him. In effect, children are introduced to the concept of living for Jesus. They are taught about his love for his world – especially as seen in the sacrifice of Jesus at Calvary – and of the worth of following his teachings.

Junior soldiers are invited to wear a uniform. Its style varies from culture to culture but it introduces the child to being identified as a Christian and is a link with the current generation of senior soldiers. As with other opportunities for children in their early years, junior soldiership is a crucial step in giving children a sense of belonging.

Junior soldiers have their own activities. In many countries awards can be gained by following a varied and informative (though not overly demanding) course. In this way, junior soldiership becomes a training ground for life as a Christian. Rather than being left to the lottery of stumbling into their own values, children are intentionally guided into wholesome, life-enhancing activity.

There are currently more than 350,000 junior soldiers in the Army globally and hundreds of thousands of former junior soldiers who went on to become senior soldiers, subsequently enjoying a life of service for the Lord Jesus. They thank God for the benefit of their childhood training and for the early place they were given in the Army's ministry.

Not every territory and not every corps does well at introducing children to the joys of junior soldiership in the 21st century. The many legal safeguards introduced in some countries to ensure that those working with children can be trusted, have at times been seen as a further modern, bureaucratic intervention, which has discouraged some from even starting the process. Yet the safeguards are entirely in harmony with the wholesome, healthy approach to life of a movement that teaches and practises holiness.

The pace of life and the stress it brings may also discourage corps from organising junior soldier activities. It can understandably be seen as an added 'burden' in a busy schedule. Yet where junior soldiership is promoted well it is invariably enjoyed and becomes a priceless investment in each child's future. It is also an investment in the Army – with the child often bringing other family members to the corps and faith.

It took 200 years to build the main structure of Germany's magnificent Cologne Cathedral. Those who helped build it accepted the fact that most of them would never see it completed, but they were glad to be providing something of splendour for generations to come. Giving selflessly for the future is a quality which can always be promoted.

Without junior soldiership, The Salvation Army's links between generations are weakened. The infrastructure which sees one generation teaching and leading the other is damaged. No other expression of the Church has such an enterprising form of membership. This has been a long-standing success story in the Army's history. It tells children we care about them and that we want them to enjoy the faith which fires us. It is not just an optional extra in the Army's structure. Its contribution is vital. It should be used to its full potential.

For discussion

▲ Jesus felt strongly about children being moulded positively in the faith (see Matthew 18:1-6). What measures should we take to ensure that this happens and that they are protected from harmful influences?

▲ Having tried to assess who and what have had the greatest effects in moulding your life, what areas might benefit from being revisited?

▲ Discuss the dual roles of responsibility and influence in moulding children in faith for the future

▲ Discuss the emphasis and priority given to junior soldiership where you are. Consider and plan how junior soldiership can be used to its greatest effect in your corps.

Chapter 7

'Let no one despise your youth'

'Don't let anyone look down on you because you are young,
but set an example for the believers in speech, in life, in love, in
faith and in purity' (1 Timothy 4:12).

NO one should expect teenagers and young adults to be perfect. It
is unreasonable. They have experienced and learned much of life,
but there is still much more in front of them. They can't be
expected to be aware of the challenges that await them, even
though some give the impression they know most of life's answers.
They often have great ideals and sometimes when they look at
generations that precede them they express disappointment. They
may be unrealistic and wildly unfair in their judgments, but this is
only to be expected – perhaps even sometimes admired, because
they are showing they care.

When young people become concerned about particular issues
they are rarely half-hearted. They care passionately and expect
others to feel the same. They campaign for causes and challenge
hypocrisy and apathy wherever they think they have found them.
They don't like compromise or conformity. They don't expect ever
to embrace them. A different perspective on these issues usually
develops later. Now they are concerned with building lives and
careers, with forging ahead and planning the future. Other aspects
of life's realities – reflection, review, remorse and regret – seem a
long way off, if they are contemplated at all at this stage.

As they begin to taste adulthood they also discover the power to
make an impression – to change the *status quo*, to right wrongs

and put their stamp on their own generation. Some aren't so idealistic. They decide the world is there to serve them, to be used for their own purposes. Surveys of students in their late teens usually show that high in the priorities of a large proportion are to 'make money', 'be rich' or 'get on'. The number who are ready to forsake personal ambition for a life of vocation is comparatively small. Perhaps it has always been like this.

What hasn't been the same is the rapid pace of change. No other generation has lived with such unrelenting, constant change or with such a mass of information available. Because those born since 1980 have known nothing but change, they are unlikely to fear it in the way that it might unsettle older people. Change excites them. Innovation has followed invention. What was new and admired only a few years earlier is quickly and unceremoniously discarded. It is accepted that the next invention will have a comparatively short popularity span and then be replaced. But there is a negative factor for youth to negotiate – they have grown up in a 'throw away' society.

The same trend applies to employment. Whereas parents – and certainly grandparents – lived in a world where loyalty to one employer meant security and was considered praiseworthy, today's youth are expected to move from job to job to gain experience, taking up a 'better offer' when it presents itself. They are encouraged to live for today in a world that seems to them increasingly unable to guarantee a future, either peaceful or prosperous.

Developing countries also suffer at the hands of progress. When their brightest students move away to gain more knowledge or experience they cannot be guaranteed to return home to contribute their new-found skills. Apart from tasting the fruits of affluence, many choose to stay where they have good wages in order to send money home to families who depend on this income.

It would be surprising if all this didn't affect attitudes to relationships. Having seen divorce become more prevalent throughout the world, young people are either sceptical about the value of monogamy or wary about making long-term commitments. An increasing number decide to live together rather than marry. In many countries this has become the norm.

Mixed and step-families are an added dynamic in a world of constant change and adjustment. While redesigned families can bring fresh stability to young lives, there are casualties too. Some distance themselves from other members of the family, others never 'fit in' to the new set up, or feel they are unwelcome or in the way. Growing up in a fragmenting or dysfunctional family environment, many young people see each other as their most precious resource. They become 'tribal', with gangs operating as their new surrogate extended family.

The prosperity of the 21st century is another factor. Some parents have tried to 'buy' their children's affections with lavish gifts, or have given money as a substitute for spending time with them in the busy and demanding routine of life. Significantly, the fastest-growing suicide rates among the young are in prosperous nations. The streets of the capitals hide rejected, disillusioned, damaged young runaways – for whom no one is bothering to look. These too are part of the Army's family. Effectively helping them is a growing challenge.

Salvation Army youth come in all varieties. Although they are young, like other age groups, they are all at different stages of spiritual development and maturity. Some need more nurturing and encouraging than others. Others are 'born leaders' and make their presence felt. There are those who are frustrated at not being given responsibility or at being 'kept down' by older or more senior Salvationists. Some are not enthusiastic at all. They identify with the Army under protest and may be reacting to having been 'forced' to attend by their parents. There are those who have been badly damaged and don't know how to relate to others. Some give little thought to anything, including their faith. They all need love, a sense of belonging and of being valued.

Peer pressure and acceptance are significant factors in teenage life and these naturally impact on any interaction with the Army. Unmotivated or embarrassed youth will hesitate to invite their friends anywhere near the Army, whereas committed youth will want their friends to be part of the Army's youth scene. If occasions to which friends are invited avoid pitfalls – such as being 'out of touch' with reality or embarrassingly insular – then all will be well. If not, young Salvationists will feel sadly let down in their efforts to attract their friends.

This is why they are often more comfortable arranging their own get-togethers. They feel safe with them. So will their friends.

In all this they deserve understanding from older members of the corps. More than that, positive encouragement and support of their efforts will mean a great deal to them. Advice from older friends – who have all been young – can help them avoid mistakes. Not all advice is good and some is ignored, yet interaction between the generations can be enriching and affirming. Both young and old may need to be patient at times, but if each has the other's best interests at heart, positive ways forward can usually be found.

A move to university is always significant, but its implications for spiritual (and other) development are huge, as is the potential for growing away from the faith and values learned at home. Many young Salvationists never return to their home corps, some failing even to make an initial contact with a fellowship in their new area. Some corps are creatively proactive at this crucial time, ensuring as far as they can that all new students arriving in their district are contacted, cared for and warmly welcomed. But it is evident that so much more needs to be done with networking, planning and preparing for this annual exodus of gifted young people from their homes. It is essential for the Army to be on its guard against what may be its greatest potential loss – and greatest loss of potential.

Music plays a huge part in 21st century life and generations vary in their tastes. This can present problems where worship and worship styles are concerned. Traditional hymns have survived largely on the depth and content of the words – with doctrine being learned 'automatically' as they have been sung. Simple tunes were written or found to accompany them. The better ones survived. Today it is the music that counts the most. Songs with dated rhythms and archaic words are often discarded, although young people do relate to some older songs when a modern idiom is applied.

A further aspect of the relationship between generations is that older generations have at times given in to pressure and encouraged the younger ones to do what pleases them – when it would have been better to give reasons for looking at alternatives. Giving in to the temptation to be popular and fit in with 'the image' helps no one in the end. Organising only entertainment-style worship for youth rallies and get-togethers can imply that young people have little depth or capacity for discerning the things of God.

There will always be a case for enjoying worship in age or generational groups, but it is a mistake to avoid meeting together as a family of God. It is in the mutual support for that which helps each draw close to God that the love of God is expressed. Rejection or derision of each other's needs is contrary to his will. As in any family, to live together in harmony each member needs to find a balance between their own preferences and those of the rest of the family.

When the Apostle Paul told youthful Timothy that he hoped no one would look down on him because he was young, he wasn't speaking only to the older generation. He was reminding Timothy that he had a valuable contribution to give to God and his work. All youth should be encouraged to give to their potential.

For discussion

▲ 'Don't let anyone look down on you because you are young . . .' (1 Timothy 4:12). Why do you think the Apostle Paul addressed these words specifically to the youthful Timothy? Why did he follow them with 'but set an example for the believers in speech, in life, in faith and in purity'?

▲ Discuss how the world has changed in the past 30 years. Share how this has affected your generation.

▲ Identify ways in which young and old view the world. What can they learn from one another? How can they work together for the Kingdom?

▲ In what ways can the energies of youth best be channelled and used in the Army and your corps in particular?

Chapter 8

Embracing the faith

'Therefore, I urge you, brothers, in view of God's mercy, to offer your bodies as living sacrifices, holy and pleasing to God – this is your spiritual act of worship. Do not conform any longer to the pattern of this world, but be transformed by the renewing of your mind. Then you will be able to test and approve what God's will is – his good, pleasing and perfect will' (Romans 12:1, 2).

EVERY major religion has its way of recognising those who profess belief. The passing on of the faith through generations plays an integral role for those 'born into' a faith.

In Jewish Law every Jewish boy becomes a bar mitzvah on reaching the age of 13 years. This is automatic whether or not a ceremony takes place. Bar mitzvah literally means 'son of commandment' and it is assumed that at the age of 13 every Jewish boy is old enough to live by the commandments. Since 1922, a bat mitzvah ceremony has been available for girls, but this takes place at the age of 12. Girls are judged to mature more quickly.

Any child born into a Muslim family automatically becomes a Muslim, and initiation ceremonies are basically reserved for conversions. Yet it is not the ceremony but the moment when profession of faith takes place that is regarded as the actual moment when a non-Muslim becomes a Muslim. The ceremony simply bears witness to what has already been professed.

The main Sikh ceremony of initiation dates back to the late 15th and early 16th centuries. Amrit Sanskar, as it is called, was

43

introduced during the life of Guru Nanak Dev, though, as with other religions such as Buddhism and Hinduism, there are a number of initiation ceremonies, some relating to specific teachers and gurus.

The Roman Catholic and Anglican Churches are among those Christian churches that use the word 'confirmation' for the ceremony in which people are welcomed into membership. The word 'confirmation' recognises that any adult having been baptised into the Christian faith as an infant may confirm that faith through personal choice in adulthood. Confirmation is usually preceded by a series of confirmation classes.

Adherence to any religion invariably means adherence to standards of behaviour, codes of conduct and obligations before God. The Christian religion is no different in this respect, yet it is more helpful to see Christianity as a way of life. It is total identification with Jesus Christ as Saviour and Lord – with a commitment to follow him and his teaching.

Becoming a Salvationist is not just about becoming a member, or following in the footsteps of other members of the family. It is about becoming a soldier. The Army needs soldiers. It would be difficult to envisage an Army without soldiers. It needs a committed fighting force. It needs an infrastructure of people who can be depended upon – people who are 'convinced that the love of Christ requires the devotion of their lives' (as the covenant ceremony records), who make themselves available for service, and who will respond readily to human need.

We have considered in earlier chapters the importance of introducing a newborn baby into the fellowship of the family of God, and the wisdom of teaching children the Christian faith by word and example in their formative years. We have noted that The Salvation Army introduces children to following Jesus by means of junior soldiership. We have acknowledged the joy of seeing fourth, fifth, or sixth-generation Salvationists embracing the family expression of service.

But, however well the faith has been 'learned' or 'observed', there must come a moment for each individual that is utterly their own – a moment when Christ is accepted as personal Lord and Saviour. It is the defining moment. It may well be a moment when the godly influence of successive generations is seen at its best – bearing spiritual fruit – but it is essentially a moment of individual commitment to God, embracing personal belief and experience of what has been learned.

Decisions to follow Christ may be made anywhere – and they are. They are made at the mercy seat, at home, in country lanes or busy streets, among a group of people or alone, in moments of great joy or times of deep sorrow.

Many who have grown up in the faith find difficulty in identifying their personal 'moment' of conversion. Following Jesus has been a natural part of their life from earliest days – for which they thank God. There is, however, opportunity in adult life to decide to make a covenant with God. The Salvation Army makes provision for marking such decisions by means of a public ceremony in which soldiers are sworn-in.

It is because The Salvation Army was born to fight evil that it needs soldiers, not merely members. There is a part for every soldier to play in this fight, and as many parts as people. Every soldier is unique. Each person has different gifts and qualities. In his first letter to the Corinthians (12:12-27) and also in Ephesians (4:11-13), the Apostle Paul highlights the diversity of gifts and parts individual Christians may play in the work of the body of Christ. He takes up the theme on several occasions because some Christians of the time were assuming either that the part they played was more important than others or that others should be like them.

It is unreasonable – and disingenuous – to infer that every soldier should be gifted at street evangelism, for instance, or be involved in specific social programmes, or able to speak confidently in public. Using the analogy of the body, Paul writes: 'If the whole body were an eye, where would the sense of hearing be? If the whole body were an ear, where would the sense of smell be?' (1 Corinthians 12:17). In addition to its gifted evangelists, its highly-dedicated social workers and its powerful preachers, the Army needs people who know how to listen, to notice, to encourage, and to provide hospitality or baby-sitting. Some who are incapacitated may feel they are able 'only' to pray, yet their part is as valuable as any other and should constantly be acknowledged as such.

Recognition and use of one another's personality, gifts and talents foster a sense of unity and shared purpose. They also lead to a wise use of resources. It doesn't matter who plays which part if everyone is committed to a common aim – the salvation of the world.

Although many forms of service are available – leading a house group, membership of a music section, literature evangelism or caring for the homeless, to name but a few – soldiership is more than activity. It is about handing over your whole life to the control of Jesus and developing a relationship with him.

In his letter to the Romans, Paul urged his readers to 'offer your bodies as living sacrifices, holy and pleasing to God' (12:1). He then referred to doing so as 'your spiritual worship'. Salvation Army soldiers worship God, first and foremost, by the way they live. They do so best by inviting him into the centre of their lives. This is what Paul calls 'Christ in you, the hope of glory' (Colossians 1:27).

In recent years the Church has used the phrase 'incarnational ministry' to describe the kind of ministry which identifies with the poor and marginalised, coming alongside people and living among them selflessly. This kind of ministry is readily associated with The Salvation Army – from its earliest days – yet it is energised and made effective only by the 'incarnational ministry' of Christ living in the heart of each Christian. If this relationship is confirmed, with Christ leading, individual Salvationists will prove the value of Paul's promise – and know 'his good, pleasing and perfect will' in their lives (Romans 12:2).

As generation succeeds generation in Salvation Army worship and service it is the personal surrendering of our lives to God as a sacrament – Christ living in his life in and through us – that ensures the faith is both embraced genuinely and passed on effectively.

For discussion

▲ Read Romans 12:1, 2 and discuss how the whole of your life is your true worship.

▲ Share how growing up (or not growing up) within the movement has affected the way you view the Army.

▲ What are the dangers and advantages of being taught the faith throughout your youth within the security of an established fellowship?

▲ Salvation Army soldiership finds genuine expression when we embrace Paul's words and 'offer our bodies as living sacrifices, holy and pleasing to God' (Romans 12:1). Consider how Christ living his life in us is at the heart of soldiership.

Chapter 9

'Am I my brother's keeper?'

'Then the Lord said to Cain, "Where is your brother Abel?"
"I don't know," he replied. "Am I my brother's keeper?"'
(Genesis 4:9)

IT isn't difficult to detect the insolence in Cain's response to God's question, 'Where is your brother?' (Genesis 4:9). His reply implied that he assumed no responsibility for his brother's whereabouts. In truth, he knew that his brother was dead. He had killed him out of jealousy (v 8).

This sad incident followed an encounter with God that his parents, Adam and Eve, had themselves handled badly. Having been told by God that they could eat freely from any tree in the Garden of Eden – except one – they chose to eat the forbidden fruit. They had been warned that the consequences of doing so were grave (Genesis 2:17), but still they had taken the risk.

Now they were exposed and in their encounter with God, as Cain did, they chose to deny personal responsibility. Adam blamed Eve for encouraging him and Eve blamed the serpent for deceiving her (3:12, 13). In effect, they were pleading that they were not responsible for their own actions. With Cain it was different. He didn't put forward the kind of feeble excuses that his parents made. He simply didn't care!

Cain was defiant in the face of God. He challenged God's questioning and correction (4:6, 7) by deliberately acting against him. When he finally uttered the words, 'Am I my brother's keeper?' he had wiped his hands of any responsibility outside his

49

own interests. His actions had not only resulted in a tragic death, they also led to him to despair (v 13).

Denial of moral responsibility is all too familiar today. The comfort and wealth of the Western world stands in stark contrast to the poverty and needs of other societies. To add insult to injury, the poor are not only marginalised they are also often exploited by their stronger neighbours. Even the poor exploit the poor in an effort to survive. Despite efforts made by some politicians, non-governmental agencies and others, a sense of collective responsibility for our brothers' welfare seems conspicuously absent. Among those keen to 'do something' compassion fatigue sets in. The media present problem after problem, need after need, disaster after disaster – it is all too much. It becomes overwhelming.

Yet the world is beginning to wake up to some issues, such as the collective responsibility for preserving the planet's resources. Global warming presents urgent challenges and world leaders as well as the population at large are being confronted with the responsibility to think of future generations and the legacy being created for them. The Chinese proverb 'One generation plants the trees, another gets the shade' has significance in more ways than one.

Each of us also carries individual responsibility for 'our brother'. Almost every action we take affects others. In making decisions to benefit ourselves we run the risk of automatically hurting someone else. It needn't be so. Society is at its best when supply and demand result in mutual benefit.

The indulgence of the rich – luxury, drug abuse, binge drinking, 'must have' items and serial shopping – indicates that responsibility for others is largely not among their priorities.

In contrast to Cain's insolent approach to his brother's welfare, Jesus emphasised that the command to 'love your neighbour as yourself' (Luke 10:27) was second only to the greatest commandment – to 'love God with all your heart, soul, strength and mind'. It isn't possible to be a Christian and ignore our obligations to others.

A sense of responsibility for other people – needy or otherwise – is at the heart of Salvationism. People 'join up' and become soldiers (not members) of The Salvation Army to make an impact in the world. Salvationists want to make a difference – to help the marginalised, the oppressed, the poor, the unloved, the neglected and forgotten. As Jesus tells us to look for him in the faces of the needy (Matthew 25:42), Salvationists cannot ignore them and still be true to their calling. The Army family includes every person who comes with a need – as well as some for whom it has to go looking. Not every problem can be solved, nor every sense of despair overcome, but the intention and motive to care must be at the heart of our response.

A recent addition to the Army's social services ministry – the International Social Justice Commission – emphasises Salvationist responsibility to be involved strongly on behalf of the marginalised. The Army's practical social work is now joined by strengthened advocacy.

In a movement dedicated to helping others it has sometimes been said that the Army has neglected needy people within its own ranks. In times of family crisis, marriage breakdown, financial strain, bereavement or misdemeanour 'the Army' has sometimes failed to show appropriate compassion to those who previously have given their time and energies readily to others.

On the other hand there is the danger of 'favouring your own', for example when goods are donated for distribution. It is often easier to identify genuine need among the closest group of workers than to seek out others whose need may be greater.

The Salvation Army family has a mutual responsibility to encourage and support one another – in the building up of faith and in sharing the burden of service. It is an essential component. New Testament letters urge Christians not to overlook this basic responsibility (1 Thessalonians 5:12-15). It is unifying and strengthening.

In their eagerness to move the Army forward, some may have been overly hard on members of the family. Criticism, judgment and discouragement all have an undermining effect. The responsibility to avoid heaping unnecessary burdens on others – especially leaders – needs to be heeded (Hebrews 13:17).

Another aspect of family responsibility is inclusiveness. There are families within the Army family. These units are often a blessing and can be strong bases from which to contribute effectively. Even so, tensions arise when the family base is so closed that those without strong or large families of their own feel excluded or insignificant. People who live on their own or who do not automatically have the support of close friends or associates have much to offer a fellowship – but their potential contribution sometimes remains unrealised. There may be no deliberate intention to exclude. It is more likely that they are overlooked unthinkingly. Unfortunately, feelings of being undervalued or 'not fitting in' are still a reality.

The Army's internationalism is a powerful component in a divided world. Its shared aims bring together people of all races and cultures. Its unity in Christ is not only a powerful witness to the grace of God, but also gives further opportunity to be our brother's keeper. Internationally the Army has a 'Partners in Mission' programme. It is an International Headquarters initiative, but each territory or command has its own given links with others. Whereas one territory may be able to supply finance for desperately needed social projects, another may be able to respond with personnel. Many corps have links with corps from other countries. They learn from one another and have a sense of keeping the wider family of God together in purpose and mission.

Another well-established feature is the annual Self-Denial appeal in which every territory, command and corps takes part. It is mutual giving of personal finance to the growth and ministry of the international Army. No matter how poor, each unit of the Army family is invited to contribute. The sacrificial giving of those in deprived circumstances is an inspiration.

Spread throughout the world the Army has countless obligations. Millions look to it for support, nurture, safety and hope. There is always more need than the Army is capable of meeting, but Salvationists will always believe in trying to be their brother's keeper and in finding their resources in their Heavenly Father (Matthew 7: 9-11).

For discussion

▲ Look at the accounts of Adam and Eve trying to deny responsibility for their actions (Genesis 3:8-13) and Cain denying responsibility for the care of his brother. Which is the greatest challenge to us:
  a) Blaming someone else for what is wrong
  b) Feeling no sense of personal responsibility for the plight of others?

▲ How strong is your own sense of responsibility to others? How does it show itself?

▲ The needs of our world – locally and globally – can seem overwhelming. How can we make an impact where we are?

▲ The internationalism of the Army is one of its greatest strengths and a powerful witness to a divided world. How much better could your corps support fellow-Salvationists in other countries?

Chapter 10

A wider family

'You are no longer foreigners and aliens, but fellow citizens with God's people and members of God's household' (Ephesians 2:19).

IN recent years the Church has been accused of losing touch with the 'real world'. It has increasingly been regarded as 'removed' from the main stream of life and culture, its ways often being seen as antiquated or irrelevant, and its reluctance to embrace prevailing trends as 'stuffy'. The world has moved on but the Church has remained in the past. At least, that is the perception of many.

In fairness to the Church, it deals with eternal truths. If it responded to every passing fad it would lose credibility and ultimately have nothing of substance to offer. It would also find itself compromising on matters of belief and practice. It has to be discerning and selective. Whenever it 'moves with the times' it has to be sure that it does so in keeping with the Apostle Paul's intention to 'become all things to all men so that by all possible means I might save some' (1 Corinthians 9:22). Paul keeps it all in context by concluding, 'I do all this for the sake of the gospel' (v 23).

The Church must embrace Paul's passion for saving the lost. It is vital to its own well-being because it exists to bring others to faith and into relationship with Jesus Christ. It needs to be inventive, creative and, as far as possible, all-embracing in its interaction with everyone.

Yet it also needs to be acknowledged that, particularly in Europe and a number of other first world countries, millions of people have moved away from the things of God. It would be wrong to place the blame for the gap between Church and community solely with the Church. A major challenge for the Church today is that countless communities around the world that were once Christian are now largely ignorant of even the most basic facts and teaching about Jesus. They have apparently rejected Christ without ever having taken a serious or in-depth look at who he is or what he did and taught, while still enjoying the security of their country or state that has been founded on the Christian faith.

The task of welcoming such people into the family of God is made all the more difficult because the large majority are simply not interested, and in their affluence see no need for God.

This kind of indifference can easily encourage negative responses from Christians – why should we bother about them if they aren't even bothered about themselves? But to respond in such a way is to deny the commission of Jesus to 'preach the gospel to all creation' (Mark 16:15). Christians must not ignore those who show no interest, neither should they attempt to pressurise or force people into listening to the gospel – yet they are called to help people become aware of it.

Faced with such challenges and accusations regarding their own irrelevance, some Christians and churches have lost confidence in what they are and what they do. Some retreat into themselves, while others make ill-thought-through changes or become ready to follow whatever seems to be working somewhere else. In so doing they have forgotten a fundamental principle of integration.

Interviewed on UK television about Britain's rapidly increasing multi-cultural and multi-faith society, the Archbishop of York (Ghanaian-born Dr John Sentamu) spoke of the foolishness of relegating the country's long-standing Christian faith to 'just another faith' in order to achieve integration. Britain needs to retain and identify with the faith which has made it what it is, he said, and the culture which has come from it. If it doesn't do that, those coming into the country will have nothing *into which they can integrate!* The alternative would lead to lack of any meaningful national identity – and to cultural chaos.

Dr Sentamu's sentiments apply equally to The Salvation Army. It would be foolish to compromise or relegate the principles and practices on which it has been founded simply to accommodate others. If it acts with integrity and confidence, boldly being what God called it to be, it will attract people to belong. If not, it won't seem worth joining. The Army has a wealth of riches in faith, fellowship and ministry into which people may be invited to integrate.

Examples of how the Army communicates successfully with the wider community are not hard to find. In places where the Army has 'grown up with the country' – Australia, Zimbabwe, Zambia and Kenya, for example (there are many more) – it has become part of the nation's infrastructure and fulfils numerous key roles. Throughout the world, the Army's work – with prisoners, victims of crime, people in debt, potential suicides, the unemployed, drug addicts, those with gambling or alcohol addictions, and their families – meets people at their point of need. So do many corps programmes – for the homeless or housebound, lonely or over-worked, bereaved or abandoned. The Army is best appreciated – and loved – where it carries through its role in harmony with what God intends.

Thousands of people find their way to faith through Salvation Army programmes and outreach. Whenever a life is changed for the better Salvationists are greatly encouraged and have the worth of their ministry confirmed.

Yet lessons still need to be learned. The value of 'one to one' friendship as the most effective means of evangelism is still waiting to be better understood. Spiritual campaigns have their place and can be used to help people make decisions to follow Jesus, but it is genuine friendship – seeing the gospel evidenced in someone else's life – that encourages non-Christians to believe. This kind of contact may not be part of a corps' official programme, but such everyday ministry is vital – and should be highly valued.

While it is legitimate and worthwhile for the corps programme to provide activities that enrich and benefit the lives of its regular attenders, at the heart of all that takes place there must be deliberate intention to attract those who don't yet belong – and to make them feel welcome on arrival. Unfortunately, because of the overuse of Army terminology and abbreviations, or by assumptions that 'everybody knows' a song that is spontaneously included, newcomers can easily be made to feel like 'outsiders'. Surprisingly, even the most passionate evangelists still make basic mistakes such as these, which do little to encourage people to return.

Interestingly, United Kingdom research on a divisional basis has shown that any personal welcome given by a corps officer, while appreciated, is less significant than being welcomed by members of the congregation. The officer is 'expected' to do this; other members of the congregation extend a welcome because they are perceived to *want* to do so!

There is a further barrier that arises for those from outside who look to join the Army family. It is that of a close knit community that feels threatened and reacts fearfully once a newcomer is ready and wanting to take some prominent responsibility in the corps. This is when established family members need to see further than their own interests and contribution – and ensure that their reactions are in harmony with God's will.

The New Testament shows that while the first Jewish Christians were glad for non-Jews to embrace the faith, they had difficulty in adjusting to the significance of 'sharing' their God with others. As his chosen people their role had been identifiable. The valid and equal role of Gentiles in building up the Church brought conflict and called for emergency resolutions (Acts 15:1-35). A council was called at Jerusalem in which James summed things up: 'It is my judgment, therefore, that we should not make it difficult for the

Gentiles who are turning to God' (v 19). It is just the right kind of advice for Salvationists today.

In the same way that the early Christians had to avoid a sense of 'us' and 'them' within the body of Christ, so Salvationists must be careful to ensure no sense of being patronised is felt by those they initially help. The early-day Army sang to the public of coming 'to do you good'. While it was true in its context, where such attitudes persist they can discourage others from feeling they can ever fully belong. Today, people in poor countries frequently ask their richer neighbours not to come bearing gifts but to come ready to listen to, and work with, them in mutually-beneficial projects.

As we contemplate making room for the wider family to know and enjoy the love of God, Paul's words to the Ephesians should be our aim: 'You are no longer foreigners and aliens, but fellow-citizens with God's people and members of God's household' (2:19).

For discussion

▲ Some Christian Jews didn't find it easy to welcome Gentiles into faith (Acts 15:1-11). What discriminatory barriers might the Church be putting up today?

▲ In what ways are you ready to become 'all things to all men' in order to help others into faith?

▲ What are the reasons for the gulf between Church and society? Discuss whether some cultural differences are inevitable.

▲ What improvements does our corps need to make in order to help members of our wider family feel at home? What shouldn't be compromised?

Chapter 11

'Two become one'

Jesus replied … "But at the beginning of creation God 'made them male and female'. 'For this reason a man will leave his father and mother and be united to his wife, and the two will become one flesh'. So they are no longer two, but one"' (Mark 10:5–8).

FOR the past 4,000 years – from generation to generation – marriage has generally been accepted as the bedrock of civilisation and society. The union of man with woman, caring for and nurturing any children who may be born as a result, has been regarded as a natural and integral part of human order. The participation of other family generations in the upbringing of the children has also been part of that order. In some cultures parents play a major role in selecting their offspring's spouse.

There are many variations on what constitutes a family yet, essentially, the commitment of one man to one woman has survived because without ordered commitment society breaks down. History teaches that when personal responsibilities are avoided, or when self-indulgence and permissiveness take over, stability is lost. As integrity in relationships has broken down, the infrastructure of communities, and subsequently nations, has collapsed.

Today marriage is under threat. In countries where, previously, couples have traditionally chosen to be legally married there is a trend towards cohabiting. In some societies, the preferred option is to live together rather than marry, or to cohabit until the couple feel ready to marry. In other cultures living together has been the accepted pattern, with a couple marrying once it is apparent that the woman is able to bear children.

Divorce is still largely unknown in some cultures – in India there is only a one per cent divorce rate – but in the United States of America, the United Kingdom and Australia, divorce rates are on average in excess of 40 per cent. Divorce rates for second marriages are invariably higher, with the USA recording between 60 to 70 per cent of failed second marriages. But divorce, with its challenges to give adequate care for the children involved, isn't necessarily the only or major challenge for this generation.

The concept of man with woman being the appropriate union no longer applies in many societies. Men and women living in committed 'same sex' relationships have become widely accepted. Children are now intentionally placed in the care of 'same sex' partnerships by local authorities. In addition, provision is made for women in such partnerships to be artificially fertilised and to give birth. Men in partnerships are permitted to adopt children, providing them with a home and an upbringing. Such arrangements were unthinkable only a few years ago.

The make-up of family units as such is not the subject of this chapter. For now we are merely noting that the circumstantial mix of family units – including lone or estranged parents, the widowed and step-families – add to the challenge of ensuring the well-being of all involved.

For the purposes of this chapter we are noting that not only do facts show that the sacred biblical concept of man and woman becoming 'one' is not being embraced, in many cases it is not entering people's thinking.

The creation story is clear in its concept. God ordained sexual union between man and woman, who were to 'be fruitful and multiply' (Genesis 1:28). When Jesus was questioned, or when he taught about marriage, he acknowledged the reality of divorce (Matthew 5:32 and 19:3–9), but he also took the opportunity to emphasise the sacredness of 'oneness' (19:5). Although largely overlooked, when embraced, this concept brings value and stability both to relationships and society.

Marriage brings permanence to love. It provides moral and emotional stability for parenthood. It teaches loyalty and mutual commitment. It is covenantal rather than contractual. It is accepting of the needs of the other person and expects to fulfil a complementary role to the wife or husband's life. The fact that no-one is perfect adds weight to the reason for marriage. If any spouse (incredibly) was perfect he or she would have no needs to be met! The other spouse would be redundant – simply not needed.

Marriages sometimes founder when one spouse finds it difficult to adjust to the inadequacies of the other. They also fail because of unfaithfulness or unkept promises, or because one partner realises they have made a mistake or were tricked. When marriages fail, those involved are further damaged if the Church responds only with rejection. Sadly, on some occasions, in a couple's greatest hour of need, those who should have been their main support and guide have failed to respond at all.

Scripture commanding legal marriage is not easy to identify. Marriage to one person was largely taken for granted. The seventh commandment – to not commit adultery – assumes marriage to one person (Exodus 20:14). When the Apostle Paul instructed Timothy on the disciplines expected of a church leader he emphasised that he must be 'the husband of but one wife' (1 Timothy 3:2). It is likely that the same monogamous requirement would have been expected of all.

Perhaps it is the moral disciplines required of Christians in a postmodern era that provide the greatest heartache among Christian families and fellowships. Church leaders and parents need wisdom, grace and the 'patience of Job' to know how to counsel their children who find themselves immersed in cultures where such disciplines are rare.

Those who argue that a 'piece of paper' certifying the legality of a marriage is not the most important aspect of the union may well have a form of argument, but have more likely missed the point.

The most important aspect of marriage is the sacred commitment made by the couple to one another under God – and the genuine intention to keep it. This is best done not by drifting into living together but by sharing in covenant with each other in the presence of their Christian family, and sealing it with legal commitment.

Marriage preparation classes, usually provided by the corps officer or the officer conducting the wedding, are designed to help the couple prepare for life together. The differing expectations each will bring from their respective family lifestyles need to be acknowledged, as do issues such as finance, children (or their absence) and careers, that are at the heart of all marriages. Informal discussion of this kind can be invaluable.

There are also wider challenges. With so many of the population giving such commitment very little thought, the standards of the Church may seem unreasonable and unwarranted. Yet the Church (and the Army) exists to relate to everyone. If it wants to do this successfully it must start where the people are in their thinking and attitudes, offering counsel and guidance when requested or required.

Whatever else it does the Church has to avoid creating barriers when people are first moving towards faith in Jesus Christ. It has to tread a path of integrity and principle, alongside one of acceptance and love. The fact that the Church sometimes fails in this can be because its people have become institutionalised in their thinking. Removed from the realities and disadvantages experienced by some, they neglect to use the grace of God, failing to trust him to find ways through.

Ever since its inception The Salvation Army has valued the

shared ministry of husband and wife. The spiritual partnership of husband and wife – both within and outside officership – has been one of the Army's strengths. The spiritual enrichment which comes in sharing Christian ministry is a special privilege. It doesn't happen by accident and will only develop if the couple intentionally turn to God in ongoing united relationship. Daily devotions, shared conversation about the things of God and spiritual care of the wider family all play their part in making such marriages successful and blessed by God.

Ultimately, it is through the presence of the Lord Jesus Christ in a marriage – when it is evident that it is his love that unites – that two truly become one. One in him and one with each other.

For discussion

▲ Jesus described people in a marriage as 'no longer two, but one' (Matthew 19:6). In today's world of individualism and equality, how should this be understood and lived out?

▲ In what ways can the fact that none of us is perfect play a positive part in building relationships?

▲ 'Marriage gives permanence to love. It provides moral and emotional stability for parenthood. It teaches loyalty and commitment. It is covenanted rather than contractual.' Discuss.

▲ Discuss how Christian values on marriage can be upheld while ensuring everyone feels cared for and fully accepted within the corps.

Chapter 12

Stretch marks

'Let us fix our eyes on Jesus, the author and perfecter of our faith'
(Hebrews 12:2)

MIDDLE years can be a minefield. They can be the most productive time of life, yet they can also be the most burdensome. They are neither about the beginning nor the end. They are years in which the choices of our youth and early adult life are having their effect. If those choices have proved to be misguided – or simply wrong – there is inner pressure to make fresh decisions. More than likely, however, any new decisions would affect others who have now become an integral part of our life. Every scenario is different, but every scenario needs to be managed.

Experts in the health services generally shy away from using the term 'mid-life crisis' these days. They suggest that a review of your life should be a natural occurrence – that there would be something wrong if each of us didn't take stock of where we are, what we are doing and where we ought (or would like) to be going.

Even so, it is more than likely that any review would be prompted by some dissatisfaction. It could be that life has come to a 'full stop', with either career or marriage ending. A contrasting scenario would be where pressures from too many commitments are causing stress and anxiety. The strain may be unbearable, or unworkable. A further possibility is where a single person, who would like to have married, sees time running out. A lonely future may be contemplated. Added to this, although medical science offers some alternative means of having children at a later age, the reality of the 'biological clock' ticking can also bring underlying tension.

In the main they are busy years. Physical powers are usually still good. Energy is expended on ensuring success at work in order to guarantee financial and home security. Provision for retirement has to be considered, along with many other financial commitments. These vary (sometimes dramatically) from culture to culture, but they are a reality.

For a growing family, materials for keeping children equipped for school and up-to-date with the latest technological aids for leisure and study add to the financial burden. Children have their emotional needs too. Problems at school or adjustments with puberty call for parental reassurance and support. Teenage children with examination deadlines and peer pressure may need special patience and understanding. It is often not an easy time for parents, who may be baffled by their children's mood swings and unpredictability.

At the other end of the age scale, the middle years could well bring added concern about the health and general well-being of aging parents. Extra visits and contact may be needed. Whereas previously parents gave strong support, that support is no longer there to the same extent; instead they become increasingly dependent on their sons and daughters.

Another factor is that in most western households, both spouses are in employment. At the turn of the century in the United Kingdom more than 70 per cent of mothers were in paid employment. The demands on mothers who work and also take the main role in organising the home – and find time to share in their husband's concerns – can be overwhelming.

Every household will organise itself (or not) and allot responsibilities to its members, but however they are shared it has to be acknowledged that far too many homes are under too much pressure. There is no room left for emergencies. If one person in the mix becomes too demanding – for instance, through illness, uncooperative behaviour or an unanticipated major issue –

everything else becomes adversely affected. Parents, in particular, are frequently being stretched in all directions.

This is also the time when physical and mental powers, combined with growing life experience, provide the ideal setting for achieving ambitions. It is not helpful if time seems to be running out, with opportunities for personal fulfilment going with it.

The last thing Salvationists in mid-life need is for the Army to add to their pressures. If they have managed to stay committed through these demanding years – and many don't – the Army should be the place where enrichment, strength and spiritual refreshment are found. Ideally, the Army should play a major supportive role.

With its historical inbuilt sense of commitment, the Army expects to attract people who are not afraid of hard work or serious involvement in its mission. In previous generations, when most social interaction took place at the Salvation Army hall, including many evenings, a sense of loyalty and duty grew as well. There was much that was commendable and healthy about this in the setting of the day. Society has changed in the way it interacts. Alternative commitments, at home, school or work, make their impact and the Army has, as always, needed to make adjustments to accommodate the needs of the age.

It is vital that Salvationists don't fall into the trap of judging each other's commitment by their frequency of attendance at the corps. Opportunities for living out our faith exist wherever we are and the need to diversify in order to influence more people is part of modern strategy. The most important underlying factor is that

Salvationists are faithful and true to their principles in every situation.

It is possible that, because of busyness, some people never get round to actually organising their lives. They rush from one obligation to another without managing to work out their priorities. Parents trying to keep young children quiet in meetings may not only often experience intense frustration but also find it impossible to gain any spiritual benefit from the worship. Although many may survive this lifestyle it is unlikely to be fulfilling or give a sense of well-being.

The Army could help with these challenges. Most significantly it could keep refining its culture of duty. We each have responsibilities one to another and a sense of duty itself is both worthy and biblical (Luke 17:10). It is also necessary for the Army to function effectively. Without a sense of duty the infrastructure which supports the mission collapses. Letting one another down needlessly isn't a virtue – but damage is done when leaders (and others) turn duty into a chore and make it the 'end' rather than the 'means'. In recent years, many corps have become more understanding in their expectations. They do not demand unerring attendance at rehearsals or meetings, bearing in mind other life commitments which are part of family life or work patterns.

Through the years the Army has appreciated the worth of quietness and spiritual reflection for feeding the soul. It has increasingly set aside time with God for the refreshment of officers, soldiers and friends. The value of such events is seen in the renewal of purpose and spiritual strength which is gained. Salvationists in their middle years are frequently among those who don't manage to attend spiritual retreats or days set aside simply to be with God. The very busyness for which strength is needed is usually the reason which prevents them from being there.

Yet the contribution of those in middle years to the spiritual life of the fellowship can be particularly perceptive and valuable. As they give so they receive. Those who participate not only energise others but are energised themselves. Ways have to be found for this to happen. Time to prioritise is vital.

Because these are middle years of life it is easy to lose the way. The early years of surrender to the will of God and promises made can be a distant memory. The end of the Christian journey still seems a long way off. This is a time when faults and flaws can no longer be excused as the inexperience of youth. Life has to be lived in the 'here and now' with responsibilities spread in all directions. The possibility of making little spiritual progress through these years is real.

The start of the race has promise. The last part has the reward of the finish in sight. The middle needs special attention. The writer to the Hebrews encouraged his readers to keep the total race in perspective: 'Let us throw off everything that hinders and the sin that so easily entangles, and let us run with perseverance the race set out for us. Let us fix our eyes on Jesus, the author and perfecter of our faith . . .' (12: 1, 2). It is particularly good counsel for this often overworked generation.

For discussion

▲ The writer to the Hebrews advised 'Let us keep our eyes on Jesus, the author and finisher of our faith' (12:1). List ways in which Christians can keep the priorities of their faith during the demanding middle years of life.

▲ If you have lived or are living through the 'middle years', share your experiences. What are the stresses? How might other age groups help?

▲ Discuss the wisdom of 'taking stock' of life during the middle years. What factors might make people feel they reach a crisis point at this time and how best can such crises be negotiated?

▲ Every corps needs committed soldiers. Those in their middle years have much to offer. How can the needs of the corps and the needs of the individual be successfully balanced?

Chapter 13

'And become mature'

'So that the body of Christ may be built up until we all reach unity in the faith and in the knowledge of the Son of God and become mature, attaining to the whole measure of the fulness of Christ' (Ephesians 4:12, 13).

THE elderly are on the world's agenda in a big way. In many countries life-expectancy is increasing with a consistency that is troubling both societies and governments. Not only is care of the elderly – and the resources to achieve it – a major issue, but also as people live longer their physical and mental needs increase. The elderly bring with them the limitations of age and an increasing degree of infirmity.

Countries where life-expectancy is not much more than 40 years face issues that are subtly different. For example, in some communities there is a noticeable absence of older people. The few who remain may be expected to care for their children's children – perhaps orphaned through HIV/Aids. The elderly are unlikely to be as well-educated as the children in their care, and if those children themselves have contracted HIV/Aids, their elderly carers are unlikely to have been taught the specialised skills needed. The elderly – who have been revered and cared for in other generations – now find themselves in unexpectedly demanding circumstances.

Africa and Asia are continents where reverence for the aged still exists, but circumstances have been changing in recent generations. In many places the emotional well-being of elderly people, and their housing, transport, health, security and sanitation needs, have become more problematic.

In countries where people are living longer the number of generations living together in society is higher than ever. With younger generations tending to have different interests and priorities, and the pace of life working against family social gatherings, the elderly often find themselves removed from what is going on. Alternatively, they may find themselves on the receiving end of a variety of age-related social activities, coupled with the opportunity to enjoy increased leisure time.

During the 20th century, discipline increasingly relaxed as attitudes in society became less respectful of authority and blatantly defiant of imposed authoritarianism. Post-modernism has brought what Dr Jonathan Sacks, in *The Dignity of Difference*, calls 'the disappearance of "I ought", and its replacement by "I want".' This change has profoundly affected how the generations understand each other.

Even so, a less formal approach has gradually developed between generations. Now, in many societies, it has become acceptable for children to show playful disrespect to their parents – such as sending a 'cheeky' birthday card – or joking with their teachers at school. This behaviour would have been unthinkable to previous generations and the wisdom of it is still questioned in many cultures.

Television companies have caught the mood of the age and produced programmes under the humorous titles of *Grumpy Old Men* and *Grumpy Old Women*. These programmes intentionally highlight the problems of generational differences by the perceived marginalisation of those who, as older people, feel either taken for granted or condescendingly patronised. Most of this is seen as harmless fun, opening dialogue between the generations, but when older people allow bitterness or disappointment to dominate their thinking and attitudes they do themselves no favours. An anonymous 17th century writer concluded: 'A sour old person is one of the crowning works of the devil.' Emotional maturity doesn't necessarily come with age.

For the most part, the elderly have accumulated resources of one kind or another. If it isn't in goods or wealth, it could be in wisdom and knowledge – in understanding life's problems and opportunities. If they have a mind to do so, those of mature years can use their maturity for the good of all.

In recent years, Salvationists of mature years have made themselves available for full or part-time Salvation Army service. An increasing number have retired early (from 50 years upwards) from secular employment. Having seen the need for vital work to be done they have embarked on a new 'career'. Many speak of their delight and fulfilment in using their later years in some special way in God's service.

Conversely, there are others who, in an ever-developing Army, feel they no longer have a part to play, or have even felt driven away. Some have shown a lack of maturity for their age and become upset when activities they once enjoyed are no longer available. A lack of depth in their spiritual experience can become evident at such times, but it would be unfair – and wrong – to attribute these attitudes to all who have felt marginalised.

In an earlier chapter we considered the varied needs and tastes of different age groups. We discussed the opportunity for the total family to share in offering mutual support for drawing each other close to God. When people of mature years find they are being deprived of worship settings which have enriched and strengthened them for service they cannot help but feel bereft. It is little short of an insult to expect them to adapt to approaches which best suit other age groups. A sad feature of the early 21st century is the number of mature Christians who speak of 'crying inside' or having a sense of loss when they meet for worship.

They may want to draw attention to the fact that certain aspects of worship that are integral to the Army – testimony, extempore prayer, the significance of the mercy seat, holiness songs and a sense of reflection and conversation in prayer with God – are being neglected. They instinctively understand why William Booth spoke of 'meetings' instead of 'worship services'. For them, interaction with God and with others in fellowship is fundamental to what God intended the Army to be. When they see that which they regard as precious disappearing, they cannot help but be troubled.

Supporting this mature age group requires a mature approach from those who haven't yet arrived there in years. Their willingness to try to understand can play a positive part in providing a starting point from which to move forward.

As the Army family seeks to meet numerous and varied needs throughout the world, the input – practical and spiritual – of members of the older age group is invaluable. It could be strengthened so much more if, where they are marginalised, they were to be encouraged, and helped to feel they have a valid and useful contribution to make.

Opportunities for those with time on their hands and experience in their hearts to become involved, should be endless in an Army that regards its family as stretching round the world and to all people. Everywhere people benefit from being taught, supported and encouraged. The sick, the socially deprived, lonely, worn out, troubled, bereaved or disadvantaged have their loads lightened by the input of Christians of mature years and mature faith.

The potential workforce available from such people of mature years is huge. If members of this age group can intentionally be challenged and invited to share what God has given them, the work of the Kingdom will be further enhanced.

When Paul wrote to the Ephesians about maturity, he did so by emphasising the different part each person or group has to play in the building up of the body of Christ. He saw a balance of expressions of service, with each supporting each in a unity found in Jesus (4:11-13). He looked towards the day when 'the whole body, joined and held together by every supporting ligament, grows and builds itself up in love, as each part does its work' (v 16). He saw this as helping the Church 'become mature, attaining to the whole measure of the fulness of Christ' (v 13).

When all is said and done, perhaps the underlying aim of each of us (young and old) should simply be to fully grow up – in and through God's grace.

For discussion

▲ Read Ephesians 4:11-15 and discuss how Christian maturity shows itself.

▲ Maturity cannot be measured in years alone. In Galatians 5:22, 23, Paul lists the fruit of the Spirit. These are a good measure of our personal maturity. How are you faring?

▲ Attitudes to older people vary according to culture. Discuss how you perceive them.

▲ In a fast-moving world, older people can sometimes feel marginalised. How can this be prevented in corps?

Chapter 14

'From everlasting to everlasting'

'Do you not know? Have you not heard? The Lord is the everlasting God' (Isaiah 40:28).

TODAY it has become increasingly popular to trace your family tree. People have been surprised to see how much of their family history can be discovered by researching legal documents, as well as through studying old books and registers. Those whose families emigrated years ago are particularly keen to trace their family roots. Most of us like to know where we came from.

Genealogies listed in the Bible don't usually make inspiring reading, although they often contain important information. Matthew's Gospel traces the family tree of Joseph, Mary's husband, back to Abraham (1:1-16), and Luke's Gospel goes even further back (3:23-38). Because Christianity sprang from the Judaic religion, Christians feel a link through the ages with the first people to encounter God and his laws. As they look to the future, embracing the promises of Jesus (John 14:1-3), Christians also have a hope for eternity. Their Lord is indeed 'the everlasting God' (Isaiah 40:28).

Tracing your own genealogy can produce some unwelcome information. Notorious ancestors may be discovered or the family line may not be as straightforward as was once imagined. In the same way, as Christians identify with others who make up the body of Christ they are called upon not only to be forgiving of the sins and shortcomings of others, but also to remember their own need for forgiveness – from God and from other members of the Christian family.

As we thank God for individual families through whom his word has been passed from generation to generation, it is important to have a wider perspective than our own family tree. The Apostle Peter, in his second general letter, reminds everyone that the Lord 'is patient with you, not wanting anyone to perish, but everyone to come to repentance' (3:9). God's love is for every human being, not the chosen few. He has no favourite individual and no favourite family.

The privilege of belonging to the family of God, with a fellowship and unity that extends through all generations and into eternity, should help us in our ready acceptance and support of others who turn to God, also unworthy yet wanting to belong.

As we thank God for the different generations that currently make up The Salvation Army in a seemingly ever-growing number of countries, an essential ingredient of our thanks is for the part each generation plays in the family of God.

The freshness of a new-born baby reminds us of innocence and purity. It challenges us to do nothing to destroy or taint that purity. The dependant and trusting nature of infants encourages us to dare to be mutually dependent on one another's contributions, and trusting of God on whom we all depend.

In the same way that we see children take their first steps and enjoy watching their progress, so we can support those new to the faith who may not immediately be aware of the pitfalls awaiting them. Preventing unnecessary hardship or heartache is as valuable as rescuing someone who is already in trouble.

The healthy moulding of young lives is crucial. We can see why Jesus warned people about the consequences of damaging a young life spiritually (Matthew 18:6, 7). The alternative – playing a positive part in the spiritual development of a child – adds value and a sense of worth to the life of the giver. As we help mould young people for good, it is worth taking time to consider the effects our own moulding had on us. Some of it will have had a negative impact and may need to be brought to Jesus for healing.

As junior soldiers are trained in the ways of God they begin contributing to the lives of others. They encourage hope for the future and reflect God's goodness. As they become aware that God is using them they are enriched and begin to see how God can use them more widely in the future.

Teenage years are the years when young people either decide to stay within the family of God or (perhaps gradually) abandon the disciplines of the faith. Teenagers need and deserve encouragement, patience and strong support. Time given to showing them that they are valued is vital at this stage of life when so many choices have to be made.

Early adulthood, which often involves choosing a life's partner, is lived in a world which has changed vastly from that in which parents and grandparents lived. The kind of stability and predictability of home and employment which once undergirded society is frequently missing. The number of alternative lifestyles, opportunities and temptations available are subtly different and seem to have increased beyond anything that may have been imagined a few years ago. As this age group begins to nurture the next generation it will help immeasurably if it has already developed a sense of the eternal in its overall life-values.

The busyness of mid-life has discouraged many from playing an active part in Christian fellowship, yet this is the age group with the resources, energy and experience to contribute. Above all, staying in touch with God will help this generation find its way through. As for all generations, keeping open a personal relationship with the Lord, through prayer, is the key,

The significance of the part played by people of mature years shouldn't be understated. This age group has the influence and experience to build up and encourage the younger ones – of whatever age. It also has the power to prevent progress and discourage enthusiasm. Its role is crucial. Yet it has been marginalised by some, who assume it has had its day. It is important to remember that those of this generation tend to become more reflective as they move towards the latter years of their life, and many who previously have shown little apparent interest in the things of God begin to explore what faith is about. 'Like attracts like' and 'elderly' corps which it had been assumed would close as their soldiers died have done nothing of the kind. If this age group's contribution can be respected and pursued, it could be among the most effective.

Humankind has found numerous ways of paying homage when people die. The Church is built on the hope of eternal life made possible through Jesus. In keeping with its military terminology The Salvation Army refers to its soldiers as being promoted to Glory when their earthly life ends. Non-Salvationists who attend Army funerals are frequently inspired by the positive nature of such gatherings in which faith and thanksgiving have strong emphasis.

Even so, bereavement brings pain. It isn't only those who have lived for many years who die. People of all ages die and the circumstances in which they die vary considerably. The quality of ministry to the bereaved is always crucial. It demands the best that each officer or fellow-Salvationist can give. The reality of death shouldn't be avoided in conversation, nor should the opportunity to share at depth things which will be helpful to those who mourn. Care and counselling as someone approaches death are also of the utmost importance, providing never-to-be repeated opportunities for ministry to the person who is dying, as well as to relatives.

Each life, however short, touches all generations. We are all influenced by the presence of others, their actions and their place in our lives. As loved ones and friends die we become the guardians of their memory. Their influence lives on.

We are not guardians of their spirit. In this respect some cultures struggle with coming to the realisation and acceptance that there is only one mediator between God and man – Christ Jesus (1 Timothy 2:5). As he prepared to go to Heaven himself, Jesus promised, 'I am going there to prepare a place for you' (John 14: 2). Christian faith is solely in him. It cannot be compromised with superstitions or ancestral beliefs.

Christianity's underlying integral strength is its eternal link with Heaven through Jesus. In Romans 8:38-39, the Apostle Paul speaks of his conviction that 'neither death nor life, neither angels nor demons, neither the present nor the future, nor any powers, neither height nor depth, nor anything else in all creation, will be able to separate us from the love of God that is in Christ Jesus our Lord'. Through his Spirit, Jesus is with his people on earth as he is also with those who have gone before in Heaven. In him all are united. Every generation is in his care.

From generation to generation. From everlasting to everlasting.

For discussion

▲ Paul says that nothing in all creation can separate us from God's love (Romans 8:39). How well do we live in the confidence of the supremacy of his love over everything?

▲ As Jesus accepts each of us into the family of God, how well do you cope with accepting fellow Christians whom you may feel do not live up to the standards set by Jesus?

▲ Discuss your culture's attitude to death. What things hinder people from coming to true faith in Christ for their eternal well-being?

▲ By giving his life, Jesus provided eternal life for us. As a result, he has given us the supreme life-giving message for all mankind. How effectively and confidently do we communicate this as a corps?